OMAHA MAGIC THEATRE

Right Brain Vacation Photos

NEW PLAYS AND PRODUCTION PHOTOGRAPHS 1972-1992

✳

EDITED BY

Jo Ann Schmidman

Sora Kimberlain

Megan Terry

✳

PHOTOGRAPHS BY

Megan Terry

D1465293

THE OMAHA MAGIC THEATRE

1417 Farnam Street • Omaha, Nebraska 68102
402-346-1227

Front cover photograph, Megan Terry, from SOUND FIELDS, ARE WE HEAR
Cover design: Judy Shepherd

TEQUILA: A band of wild mountain wolves comes howling and barking in from the foothills.
They transform into wild women and promise to be my protectors and follow me
to the ends of the earth and that no matter how hard I work there will always be
time to party.

SAND: She lays down in the middle of Dodge Street. She does the dependable thing.
She has her frown lines removed once and for all.

FIRST EDITION
FIRST PRINTING — MARCH 1992

Right Brain Vacation Photos — New Plays and Production Photographs 1972 - 1992.
Copyright © 1992 by The Magic Theatre Foundation and Megan Terry. Printed and bound in the
United States of America. All rights reserved. No part of this book may be reproduced in any form
or by any electronic or mechanical means including information storage and retrieval systems
without permission in writing from the publisher, except by a reviewer, who may quote brief
passages in a review. Megan Terry's photographs appear with permission.

1. Dramatists - 20th Century;

2. American Drama - 20th Century;

3. Theatre - History - Omaha Magic Theatre;

4. Theatre - 20th Century - Avant Garde;

5. Theatre - Feminist;

6. Theatre - Photography;

7. Playwrights - Contemporary;

8. Theatre - Contemporary - Stage Design

ISBN 0-911382-13-5   LIBRARY OF CONGRESS NUMBER: 91-068584

Acknowledgements

WE WANT TO THANK the National Endowment for the Arts for helping to make it possible for us to publish this portfolio. Two years in the making, it represents long hours of great care but infinite pleasure for the eye and memory via flights back and forth in time.

Recognition is gratefully extended to those individuals and members of public and private foundations who have supported our work over the years. Without this support much of the work included here would not have been possible.

We wish to thank Arthur Ballet for his work with the Office for Advanced Drama Research; many of this country's early playwright-company marriages and love affairs took place because of his undying commitment to the American playwright. Also, in our fond memory of supporters are: The Ford Foundation's New American Plays Program; William L. Bradley's work at the Rockefeller and Hazen Foundations; Howard Klein and Susan Sato of the Rockefeller Foundation; Cynthia Mayeda, Dayton Hudson Foundation; The Adah and Leon Millard Foundation; Nebraska Humanities Council & Iowa Humanities Board; Nebraska and Iowa Departments of Highway Safety; Joyce Foundation; Schering Plough Foundation; United Arts Omaha; Nebraska Arts Council; and again, The National Endowment for the Arts.

Thanks to the playwrights, artists, performers, directors, designers, scholars and consultants who over the years have contributed to the artistic growth of the Omaha Magic Theatre and encouraged us to keep going.

Many others gave support in many ways. Although they all cannot be mentioned here, their energies are greatly appreciated.

Resounding thanks and appreciation:

To Omaha community members who have supported our work since 1968.

To our audiences in Nebraska, the Midwest and throughout the United States for their continued support and inspiration over the years.

Special thanks to the playwrights whose work is included here and the writers/scholars/friends who responded to the photographs.

The following individuals have provided invaluable assistance, support, commitment and creative exchange during the book project:

Carol McCabe, Professional Darkroom Services — a superb photographer and technician; her trained eye helped determine selection and size of the photographs.

Pat Kentner, Simmons Boardman Books, Inc. — for getting us started on the right track and help with the final editing.

We also thank Rose Marie Whiteley and Rob Gilmer for their dedicated work on this project.

This book would not have been completed without the excellent work and care of:

Barnhart Press

Eli's - The Separator

Judy Shepherd, Independent Omaha Graphic Designer — for her cover design

Field Paper Company

We have determined photograph placement by how one photograph relates to another, not by chronology. To know the year a work was produced at OMT, please check the Production History.

This photographic journey is funded in part through a grant from the National Endowment for the Arts. It is our hope that these photographs will serve to inspire more productions of these and other vital new works by the writers published here. Many exciting and fascinating works for the theatre have been created by these writers and their contemporaries. We hope others will be as stimulated and invigorated by these works as we have been.

Introduction

The Omaha Magic Theatre has created and produced more than 100 new plays and musicals since 1968.

We've created this book for:

THE PLAYWRIGHT — not only the playwrights represented here but for those who continue to write startling, funny, serious, daring new plays for the American Theatre.

OUR AUDIENCES and all audiences who support the art form of theatre in all its manifestations.

STUDENTS who know there is more to know than what is commonly taught.

THE THEATRE PROFESSIONAL who is hungry to see and do new work.

THE ONE who likes to look.

The following is a compilation of 156 photographs taken by Megan Terry during performances of Omaha Magic Theatre Productions and Play Events (finished productions with script in hand), 1972 - 1992. We asked scholars and theatre professionals to write responses to these photographs — to say what the play image, captured on the page, made them think and feel. Short synopses are also included, along with a few lines from each play text. You will also find narrative commentary from artists at the Omaha Magic Theatre regarding how they think about giving form to text ... what performance is to them ... how theme, character and emotion become visual situations.

We intend that this publication will reside in theatre collections, public libraries, universities, high schools and personal libraries.

We wish to serve these contemporary playwrights and their potential public by circulating news and views of their work. Information on how to contact these playwrights directly is included in the PRODUCTION HISTORY. These plays are fun to read and stimulating to produce. We hope this collection will demonstrate the powerful visual and intellectual excitement available in these works and give others the courage to produce them.

Contents

DR. C: Have you drunk milk from a cow who
has grazed on grass downwind of a nuclear
accident, however minor?

DR. C: How will history write me? A figure
in other people's stories? A voice without a
name crying out in the wilderness, or a name
without a voice, without the word that could
have saved us?

Dr. C, a modern-day Cassandra, can see the radioactive particles that affect us all. As she tries to warn the world, the pinch is put on her by Mr. Deal, a government man with a giant lobster claw for a hand. Expressionistic elements heighten our horror of the terrifying mess we're making of this earth.

THEATRES ARE NOT PRODUCING ENOUGH NEW WORK. Producers think audiences won't "get it".

Directors think producers won't let them take chances.

Playwrights are accused of writing undefined poetry — set in locales impossible to realize on stage.

We hope these photographs prove otherwise.

IN THE COURSE OF OUR WORK MEGAN TERRY LEARNED TO PHOTOGRAPH IT.
Live performance is as difficult to photograph as a puppy. Theatre is not film; it will not be frozen or posed. Theatre is special and thrilling to the viewer — when it is truly alive. A moment happens, then it's gone, never to happen precisely in that particular way again.

Megan Terry captured many of these moments.

A vision of the world self-destructing...the only thing clear — your own eyes searching for a last truth.

Catching the crumbling world in tin pans.

The horror of having someone possess your head. A tightening of the soul with one of your own hands holding the device of your own destruction.
— Migdalia Cruz

GARFIELD GOON: What happened to our cats?

JUNE GOON: Daddy said they were too dirty so he sent them away.

GARFIELD GOON: Where?

JUNE GOON: To a little town called Euthanasia.

A "Punch and Judy" slapstick horror comedy extravaganza about human aggression within the family. It poses the question, "Why do we act like goons to our children?"

JUNE GOON: You didn't notice that I cried the whole time we were moving. You didn't see how I felt about leaving that town. I'll admit we didn't have any friends, but I was attached to the lawn and shrubs.

Clean and wholesome fun for born again humanists who love originality and superwit. The theatrical innovations of Megan Terry continue to astonish and regenerate our sensibilities.
— Rochelle Owens

These images invite us to think sameness and difference together, to think past the simple opposition. Boundaries are violated here. Where does one head begin and another end in GOONA GOONA?
— Lynda Hart

An elegant, exciting gala collage of June Havoc's incredible life in the theatre. The memoir begins in vaudeville and burlesque, moves to the intense and exhausting marathon dance circuit, to Broadway, WWII USO tours, the McCarthy Hearings and her film triumphs. A marvelous retrospective of the variety of American Performance.

*Baby June is the dancing
mother of us all.*
— Jeremy Arakara

ALTERNATIVE THEATRE

It's live! It's too close! It's the truth! And the truth is always subversive.

A theatre full of surprises, new information, new ways of seeing... All theatre should be alternative — alternative to what we've learned to expect.

Our audiences enjoy expecting the unexpected. They say the new work they see at the Magic gives them new ways to use their minds and uncover feelings.

OLD AND NEW PERFORMANCE ART

Solo artists performed their work alone and/or in companies within the movements of Bauhaus, Flux, Happenings, and Contemporary Performance Art; this work has fueled our work at the Magic. Our ensemble/ creative team is made up of individual artists. Not solely theatre artists, but artists from different disciplines, gather to find the most effective way to communicate their vision.

"Do you think like you talk or talk like you think?" is the central question. Set in the heart of the family, the play is both an indictment of the sexist nature of our language as well as a hymn to the possibilities of human experience. A feral child raised by prairie dogs is found by children and brought home to be "civilized" through learning "English".

JAIMIE: The rabbit's eating our lettuce.

MOM: Is he?

JAIMIE: No. I said the rabbit.

MOM: He's eating the lettuce.

JAIMIE: No he isn't. Daddy's at work.

MOM: ...He's eating the lettuce.

JAIMIE: You're crazy!

MOM: Go to your room.

JAIMIE: If all the rabbits are boys, are all the cats girls?

This game will teach you how to talk like a girl, think like a boy and hold like a chair.
— Jeremy Arakara

IMPRESARIO: Friends, be the first in your neighborhood to observe the horrifying refinements of a master faster! Count his ribs, watch him disappear as he turns sideways. You won't be disappointed. The Hunger Artist is an artist's artist, revered universally for his sacrifice of comfort and nourishment for art.

A tender and ironic adaptation of Kafka's classic, "A Hunger Artist". People come to stare as the Hunger Artist starves himself in public. The star of a traveling circus act, he is his art. But a fickle public soon craves even more daring acts. The play asks, what is the cost of artistic integrity in this crass materialistic world?

Human desires and emotions can lead us to create our own cages, in which we celebrate our suffering.
— *Michael Skau*

THE NEW AMERICAN AVANT GARDE

Originated in the 60's, nine of the writers represented here have steadily contributed to the American theatre for 30 years.

Their older work is strong — their newer work is strong;
It does not copy the commercially successful;
It has defined its own genre.

When we present work written in the 60's back-to-back with a 90's script by a new writer, our audiences are knocked out by both. The 60's pieces are timeless and prove themselves as contemporary as the wildest new work.

Prose, so smooth and round it could be as easily sung as spoken ... about testing wings, jumping off a cliff but having someone to hold onto because you can't fly alone.

I have no idea why someone with all that glamour, like the Woman in the Window or the Lady from Shanghai, would want to get closer to God.
                                        — Ron Tavel

SHARKEY: But the wings disappeared — Folded in on themselves on either side of my backbone, Curled together like cats. And all I was left with was the face of an angel And no way to get closer to God than anybody else.

Life reflected on up-to-the-minute sunglasses is
bent forward while moving backward.

IN THE LATE 80'S WE BEGAN TO EXPLORE AND EXPLODE THE USE OF OVERHEAD PROJECTION: As a malleable, changing light source — a way to alter color or texture and completely transform the performance world.

We may now transform a stage locale from a tunnel to a field of sunflowers, to a world of lines instantly, without flying set pieces in or adding time via black-outs.

Light, image or projected text is made to interact with performer speech. Projections may magically appear on a character's forehead, over one's shoulder, or saturate a giant screen.

We project movement... Cars whiz by, clouds drift in... Subtitles juxtapose or amplify live action. We create wind... Make water stand still, bubble or churn.

This dark comedy explores with fresh, funny and incisive language the love, jealousy and fears of Lucy, a pizza delivery girl and her mother, an aging coquette. Lucy and Mother look to Milton, the stuttering victim of both their sensuous devices, for redemption — lost youth for the mother and a future for the daughter.

MILTON: I used to dream about putting her in a freezer so if I wanted to look at her face, I could just open the door and there she'd be — staring at me, eyes only for me. I remember the pain flooding her eyes as I entered her and I wonder why love and pain always come together. You fight love...but it's stronger than rope.

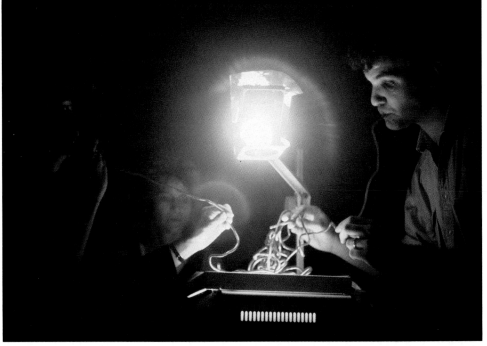

We inject Lucille Ball's DNA, instead of chocolate chips, into every set of lips. —Jeremy Arakara

A celebration of the joys of reading and writing, HEADLIGHTS is about "getting it" and imaginatively going there without boat or plane or train — on wings provided by graphic and aural combinations of sounds and shapes through the newly discovered ability to read. Aided by compassionate teachers, the protagonists acquire a skill taken for granted by most of us.

It's the secret axiom of love poetry, oration, shopping lists, and critical theory: read my words and I've touched your body.   — Elin Diamond

Literacy leads to freedom; the letter of the law means nothing to those who cannot even read letters.   — Michael Skau

If you can't read the signs, if you can't decipher the Constitution of the United States, you don't know your rights.   — David Savran

CRAIG: Don't be embarrassed by not being able to read. Be embarrassed by not tryin'.

HILARY: I wanna read music. I wanna read your letters. I wanna read the words of my songs. I wanna read you. I wanna read you my rights. I wanna read to travel. I wanna read my way inside. I wanna read.

24

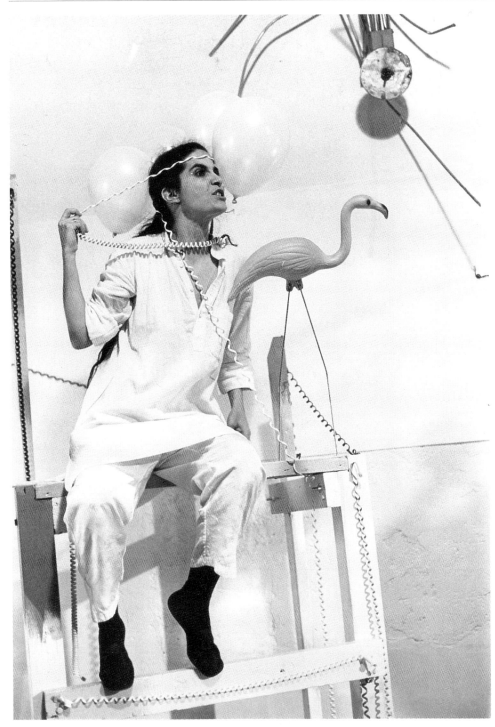

ASTRO*BRIDE: Why would you want to wear Yves Saint-Laurent eye gear? To see the poor and destitute? To see the detailed imperfection of their lives as in-focus magic realism vibrating violence?

The generation of animated clutter is one of the unacknowledged gifts of the artist. — Anon.

26

A comic, centrifugal one-person performance event that submits sci-fi language to G-Forces and comes up zany and insightful. Animated robots sing while Astro*Bride miniaturizes souvenirs of earth to take back to her native planet, Blow. An advanced anthropologist, she finds she's fallen in love with certain lesser forms of life encountered here. We meet her just as she's packing to return home for her marriage. What she takes back with her and why — what she leaves here and why — forms a hilarious and trenchant critique of our civilization. A tour de force for a comic actor of either sex.

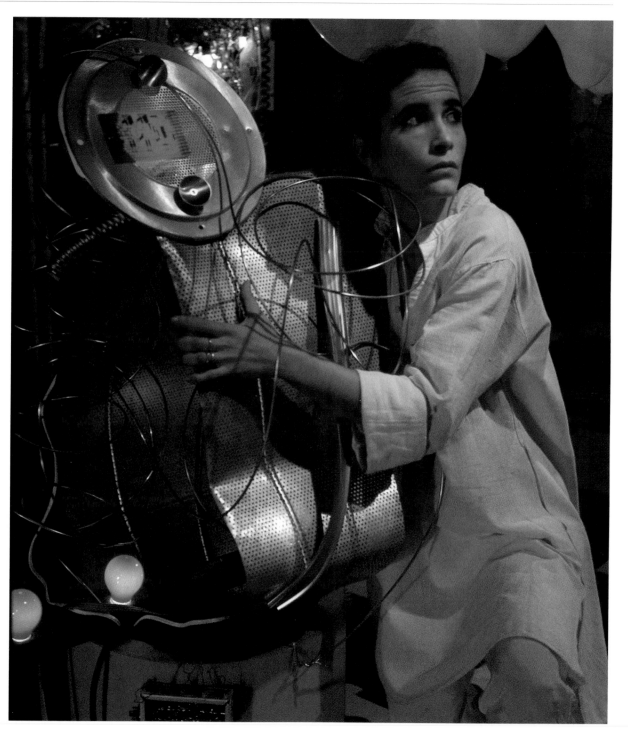

ASTRO*BRIDE: Poor Margaret Mead had to slop through swamps in New Guinea
Drag her round little body all over the South Pacific for a year
To gather the data I can spy in one hour at the set.

A woman struggles for personal independence as she approaches thirty. Running is used as a meditation and a metaphor; the runner is running toward a new and renewed love of life. Along the way she deals with her husband, her lover, her friend and her mother with the acute sensibilities aroused and honed via the practice of running.

Form follows function. Or is it the other way around? Of course I'll win. In the long distance, it's always women.
                                                   — *Susan Carlson*

RUNNER:

Pain is only physical.

I can get behind the pain. It goes away when I dream.

I'd rather have this pain in my side

than all the pains I've had in my head.

TEXT AND THEMES BEGIN THE WORK

This is true in previously scripted plays and Omaha Magic Theatre originals. Visual images, sounds and directions are then created.

The production evolves through rigorous interaction of all the art elements. A piece may begin as the look of a certain type of light ... or the shape of a room ... or the sound of insects at night.

WE ALLOW THE VIEWER IN ON THE PROCESS, by allowing them to watch the technical. As we execute a light cue, dress a performer, present a sculptural image, the technical act is also seen as performance.

RUNNER: We've got the biggest moon
    in the world
    in Nebraska,
It's gotta be — to go with our sky
That's why I run now,
I've spent so much time
    on my back
    looking at the sky —
I've turned into a prairie porpoise;
And I sing with the prairie grasses,
And I sling spit shots into spider's webs
And I must grow my arms and legs again.

PROFESSOR REVERE: Idealism is rampant. We all know what idealism is. It was brought to its zenith in the '60s in the United States of Amerikesh and produced a generation of hotheads who hotfooted it right off the map of rational thinking. While the idealist lies on her hammock strumming her lute and making love to your big toe, Toshiba is selling all our computer secrets to the Russians! Get dressed and get back on the assembly line.

I am going to come in sideways on your life and land very daintily, so maybe you'll think it was just an emerald June bug attracted by your desk lamp that settled for a second for a look-see on your nose; but I don't think you'll actually feel anything at all.   — Ron Tavel

This work celebrates courage. It's about taking and enjoying one's rightful power within the spirals we take through life. Spirals are a process not a product, presence not conclusion. The spiral of the tornado picks up everything in its path and reorders it. "I jump off the cliff and land on your feet. I jump off the cliff and land on myself!"

Because of his demands for strictly functional reproduction and strictly recreational sex, the Garden of Harry Eden quietly threatens to become hell. The author asks, "How much of yourself are you willing to give away for the sake of someone else? What price will you charge and what price will you pay?"

ADAMSON: You despise that woman.

EDEN: What makes you say that?

ADAMSON: You reduce her to her bodily function.

EDEN: She signed the deal.

I've never been good at getting that plastic wrap to cling to the sides of the bowl. Am I doing something wrong?   *— Susan Carlson*

Images of containment and exile — straightjackets, brassieres, ropes, hands covering faces, eyes, mouths, helmets, wigs, hats. Surveillance — who's watching now?   *— Lynda Hart*

The Edenic romance is rewritten, the Garden becomes a hazardous post industrial playground, its denizens disaffected and caged.   *— David Savran*

A carnival of emotional needs with conse-
quences, X-RAYED-IATE is also a theatrical
journey toward the exercise of deeper
feeling.

ROY: I was trying to get my girlfriend to marry me. For some reason I thought all I had to do was put my tongue in her ear. But that wasn't enough. She wanted me to be able to get an apartment.

BUGS: I love to see the human body with no clothes on. That's the smile of the soul.

Midwest woman sentenced for public display of anger.
— *Susan Carlson*

I'm safe from comets inside my pyramid, but space dust and sun goddesses have found the path up my nose.
— *Jeremy Arakara*

Zany images and unique language charge this
entertaining artist's comedy.

*How foolish it is to need to convene. We've been
closest together on satellites, farthest apart for
seventeen years now, and interested parties can check
out our communal clean bill of health. Why, most of
us are almost ethereal.* — Ron Tavel

LEWIS: Just a minute. I have a paragraph that pertains to the end. It says here, 'They came from every walk of life: on foot, in the air, through the sea. And when they got here they were tired and went right to bed.' The four corners of the earth were empty and the bed was full. Then trouble began. It was the beginning of the end.

40

In this bitter, modern, romantic comedy two mysterious businessmen approach two artists on a train. Attraction among these four strangers is fractured through the screen of safe sex and surreal politics.

RICK: I have three beautiful kids, with very high I.Q.s... very.
TORY: Who asked?
RICK: Old bulls make great calves.

VIVA: Not one male person moved his upper lip. Not one! Is that why all male lips disappear after thirty-seven?

Women run gauntlets exchanging their gain for pain. — Elin Diamond

MOM: I hated that store. When we walked in, one of the salesmen stared at me; I felt so uncomfortable. Why should I have to get dressed up to go spend money? I have to dress up for the office all week. On my day off, I'll be damned if I'm going to get dressed up to spend money we don't have!

HIGH ENERGY MUSICALS

All plays might be musicals. Isn't music the sounds and silences of life? An Omaha Magic Theatre presentation incorporates the jamming of sound-structure with performed word and image. Intricately composed scores and songs may also be featured. Composers and musicians have always been Magic Theatre company collaborators. We provide a public platform for their original creations.

We meet this family of seven in the middle of chaos. Their lives have been moving fast, clashing in ways that bring them to the point of disintegration. But they save themselves through discovery of the warmth and humor in effective communication.

Tuning up the orchestra to play the family romance takes more than muscle — it takes emotional strength and the ability to riff on humor.   — Jeremy Arakara

Dr. Toloon-Fraak, an obstetrician/psychiatrist has maniacal fingers in underworld drug dealings. He is hounded by his passionate wife, crazed by his young mistress, threatened by her father who is a former patient, adored by his talking dog, and spied upon by the "FEDS", who may be more than a rock group.

Anguished eyes of dirty pleasure — watched on the outside by your own second sight...

A man with a guitar sees more of your organs than you thought possible on a routine check-up. But that flashlight is so big... — *Migdalia Cruz*

46

DR. TOLOON-FRAAK: The thing I rely on is the good will of my patients. Pschug, a former patient has forgotten what we both discovered together: that the line of least existence is preferable to going out of your way. He wants to destroy my reputation, but let him beware, I have none.

KERMIT: I don't want
to be a whole person,
I just want a job!

FATIMA: If you Westerners were truly as health-conscious as you say you are, you'd be squatting. Sitting and standing up straight is military bullshit, upper-class bullshit.

A satirical look at contemporary university campus life, where earning has taken a priority over learning. Explores with bite, wit and insight, the clash between careerism and the life of the mind.

You really have to have your hand on things but every time you do, it comes off. So then you call for a council and get the jitters and act silly. — Ron Tavel

MS. HIGGENBOTTOM: Some people are sitting in apple pie order, but some people are sitting like a poached egg running down its toast. You poached eggs know who you are. Hey all you King's Horses, all you King's men come put the poached eggs into apple pie order again.

Everybody here looks either like Julie or Mario; or Anna or Augosto; or Bill and maybe Michael with a beard that I don't recognize. But any and all of them always did O.K. so I'm not one bit worried.
— Ron Tavel

A musical burlesque revue sending up the
concepts and practice of morality.

A musical game show where the contestants try to win intimacy with themselves, the other contestants, and the emcee.

CONTESTANT #1: The cops are beating the kids.

CONTESTANT #2: That girl looks just like Susan Spiegelglass. She's in Chicago and the cops are beating her.

CONTESTANT #3: Look, there's Paul Newman.

CONTESTANT #2: The cops are beating Paul Newman.

CONTESTANT #1: This can't be happening on American television. But there's Walter Cronkite.

We spend our lives trying to understand ourselves and others; luckily, we're never very successful in this effort.
— Michael Skau

A performance piece about modes of religious practice ranging from worship, through T'ai-chi to loving dogs.

THE MEDITATORS: God doesn't need repetition, but I do. God is the supreme repeater. Look at the map. See the grass. There are the rivers repeated, there are the bluffs repeated, there are the leaves on the ground. The birds will repeat in the spring. God has repeated the rings and moons around Saturn, all the planets, the stars, the clouds. Open a pea pod and eat the repeats. I am, myself, one of God's repetitions. You look similarly repeated — only in outline. I don't wish to insult your uniqueness.

IMAGISTIC THEATRE

Scripts are read. Plays are seen. Theatre is a "visual art". Performed words generate images in audience's heads. Sculptural imagery may amplify or oppose words or ideas conveyed by the script.

Alternate points of view, variety of feeling, are offered to the audience.

TOTAL THEATRE

Each artist makes a statement about the ideas of the play via that individual's discipline. Each element is as important to the whole as any other element. Theatre is text, directorial image, light, music, dance, design and architecture. Theatre is also the sound of footsteps — and silence. Each of the disciplines, which together are theatre, serve the production, the whole, as it is performed for an audience.

EXPERIMENTAL THEATRE

Experimenting begins in workshops and continues through rehearsals — before the audience arrives. We rehearse and rehearse. We rehearse as diligently as a precision drill team to get the work ready to meet the audience. We never experiment in front of an audience. We play in front of them; we interact with them.

A journey play on light that beams through walls of the psyche. About the struggle to be free from limitations of society, family expectations or from personal doubts about one's self-worth or ability. UNCHAINED suggests ways to break free of these constraints and live in more positive modes. It includes material from some of the best work created by the Omaha Magic Theatre, 1968-1988.

*How do you break free of the past? How do you
leave your father's house? How do you lighten your
burden? How do you quench your desires? How do
you take up residence in a room of your own?*
— *David Savran*

WORK ON A NEW PIECE

As a creative team we discover new things and invent new ways to share the secrets found with an audience. It's our task to see through to the truth, then to communicate the truth identified via performed imagery. As distinct voices, the playwrights, director, designers, performers, musicians are confidants to each member of each audience.

The extraordinary theatre we've been creating in Omaha for twenty-four years is not new, really — It's not far out, really — It's not dangerous, really — It's text and visuals fully realized — It's play — fully performed. We play with one another, with our audiences, with ideas, images, situations, relationships.

Theatre's been around a long time. Theatre's the art form which combines all other art forms. This abundance performed can make the poor feel wealthy. A wealth of feelings and ideas projected through stories with strong action images is why the Greek masses sat and Elizabethan groundlings stood for hours cheering-on or talking-back in passionate relationship with live performers. Traditionally, theatre is spectacle.

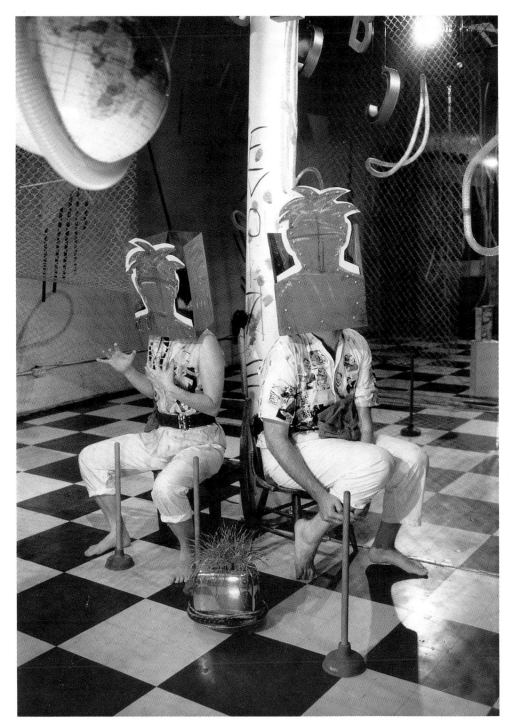

MATT: There's this room I want to get to know. I'm starting by feeling out the floor with my bare feet. Walking in that room I stubbed my toe on my tongue but was healed by the air moving through me.

The making of an avant-garde movie in this hilarious 'kitchen from hell' demonstrates, as Tavel says, "We've passed beyond the absurd, our position is absolutely preposterous."

MIKIE: I said I went to a shower this afternoon, Jo.

JO: Oh, how nice.

MIKIE: Yes, it was nice.

JO: What happened at the shower, dear?

MIKIE: I had sex with someone in the shower.

JO: With the water running?

The destruction of inanimate objects lets us know who's boss — we still watch to see if they cry as their glass eyes hit the toilet bowl brushes.
Dead Men in our laps, floating on a rubber tube over kitchen tiles — wish we were there...— Migdalia Cruz

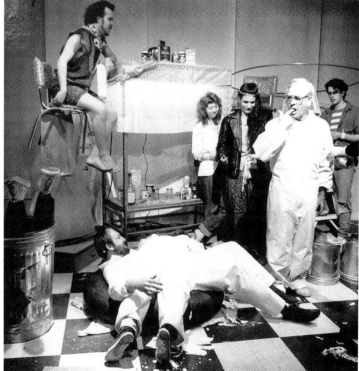

Process Oriented Work

The production (a product) always results, but focus is on the daily evolving "details" of the creative process. Absolute attention is paid to detail. The reward sometimes may be big box office; but the prime goal is the growth of each artist, through stronger collaborative and communication skills: artist to artist, artist to medium, artist to audience and medium to audience.

This performance piece plays with time and its effect on humans.

ZENA: There will be a continuous resurrection of billboards flashing neon saying: TIME HAS BEEN ERASED: THERE IS NO MORE TIME. Parking meters will be replaced by fountains of youth.

I can't figure out why I keep seeing that leonine carapace in every other Fourth Dimension or so that I pass through. But I'm looking great, so if you think it concerns me in the least, you're wrong again.
                                                                    — Ron Tavel

A (male): I finally saw, with sparkling fire and huge popping eyes amidst labor cries, like a cloud-gowned Taoist hermit, the face of my own foetus... developing very slowly and surely into a hairy spider, and a rather big one at that and one they were sure to stomp on as soon as they caught sight of it...

A young man journeys back to pre-birth then to post-birth as he discovers he's really a spider child from Brooklyn. Brilliant language and incisive theatrical images invoke the memory of the patience of waiting to be born — the supreme patience of biology — the super surreal patience of the artist.

Bizarre and vividly philosophical, Ronald Tavel disarms the audience with an inventiveness that is distinctly avant-garde. His language is comic and mysterious at the same time. — Rochelle Owens

ALFRED: Do you love me? It's not like we're putting our love on the agenda of some corporation's board meeting to be argued back and forth, subject to practical and insensitive qualifications, like if the bottom-line of your loving me meets the quota programed into your life's potential yields...

Alfred and Omeda spend a weekend at a cabin in the Rockies where they meet terror from a mysterious giant, then terrorize themselves when they unravel the string of their relationship. As the lovers unwind from one set of games and fantasies, they plunge into another.

Soul wrestling face-to-face with no referee — the loser has to reveal his most secret fear first.
—Jeremy Arakara

A multi-media theatrical performance piece about revealing oneself to oneself. It's also about how we censor ourselves to protect ourselves and others, to control ourselves and others. Many have found it necessary to bite tongues and/or close eyes and ears to censor themselves in order to get ahead on the success ladder.

BODY LEAKS examines the ways we stop ourselves from becoming what we might become — things we don't say and should, things we'll never do and could. It's about the true self being kept quiet by the projected jacketed self. Will we become victims of censorship or will we use insight to grow stronger and fortify our ideals?

Three talking heads and one silent fascist. — *Anon.*

Hysteria is the body's horrible theater. — *Elin Diamond*

SABRINA: I'm convinced you're the right formula to take my left brain on vacation.

IRENE: Feet first we burst from eminent sheets where you'd aroused my interest on purpose.

KRYSTAL: I won't let myself say anything nice, so I'm not talking.

KRYSTAL: I get confused who's who - am I me? Are you you?
It's funny, I see me looking out when I look at you.

FRED: More coffee, Ma.

MOTHER: You've had your last cup, honey.

FRED: I love coffee.

MOTHER: You'll have to drink beer now, sugar. It's cheaper. You'll like it. If you drink just the right amount of beer you can have even more fun with your bunnies.

FRED: I love you, Ma. I really love you.

Mother (played by a man) and her three jock sons (played by women) gather around the TV to wallow in football. During the course of the game the family eats, drinks, argues and overindulges while sexual politics stands on its head and consumerism kicks field goals.

Captain Mother bowls his football down videoid throats.
— Jeremy Arakara

New Performance, Image People

The work is, as we develop and present it, a vehicle for actors: actors as storytellers, as witnesses or confessors, as dancers, as moving sculpture, actors as bearers of headdresses and breast plates, actors as technicians who move set pieces, hold up a branch when a tree is called for, or present a placard if a subtitle is part of a scene.

The Wonders of Limitation

Our theatre is approximately 20' x 100', with 15' ceilings, no wings, no traps, no fly gallery. We've learned to fly ourselves and objects without wings. Imagination may enter or escape any trap.

The ceiling is fuchsia, the floor black and white checkered. Only twice have we raised the stage. Audience-performer configuration is flexible — re-thought for each production according to the demands of the work. An Omaha Magic Theatre performer is always able to look directly into the eyes of each audience member. Audience sits in swivel seats they may turn in any direction.

The two large front windows, facing the street are used to stimulate audience walk-by interaction via posted writing and visuals. This dialogue is most intense during new work development. Our windows may include performers and/or mechanized objects.

This genuine sixties gem takes a fun-house look at modern life and love, sexual repression and narcissism. Step right up! Admission only 10¢ to the eternal battle of the sexes.

HANNA: Oh, my name is Hanna O'Brien. I'm from Springfield, Illinois. I come from good middle-class American stock. My father was Irish-Catholic, and my mother Russian Orthodox-Jewish. And between the Knights of Columbus and the Hadassah meetings — Oy Vey, Maria! — were we kids confused!

The new sexual "politics": the candidate's handlers run final tests in preparation for her big night out.
— Susan Carlson

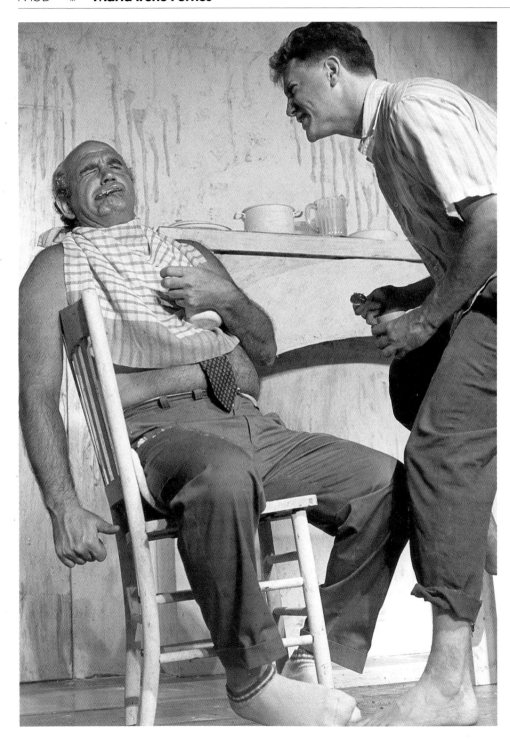

MAE: I'm going to die in a hospital. In white sheets. You hear? Clean feet. Injections. That's how I'm going to die. I'm going to die clean. I'm going to school and I'm learning things. You're stupid. I'm not. When I finish school I'm leaving. You hear that? You can stay in the mud.

A young woman, Mae, and two men live together in a house that is slowly sinking into mud. The woman struggles to rise from this environment through learning to read and think for herself. Spare and insightful language illuminates Mae's search for meaning and autonomy.

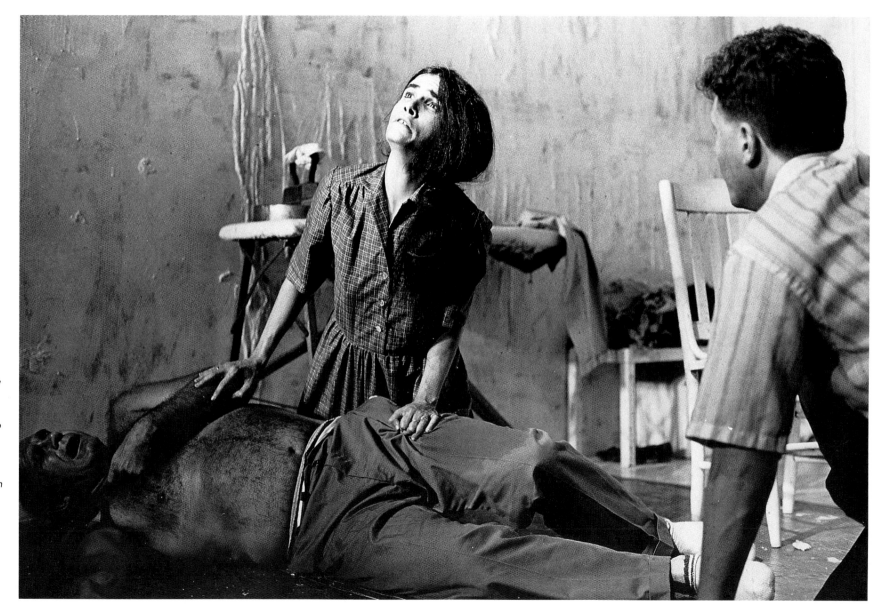

Reading and writing are the most precious of skills, they allow one to communicate, to love, to remember the past, to transform the future, to be lifted out of the mud.
— David Savran

BUSH: Midnight dumping expeditions, it's not an easy way to make a living. Drivers! Villains! When thy horns honk my bones clank! Let us join together our shuddering loins and dump on the city! If my wife had a turkey in the oven I'd give her bottled water to drink.

A "toxic waste entrepreneur" runs his illegal business out of a trailer with his wife's young lover, Nita. The moral base of this play is Owen's knowledge that there is no moral base to her characters' actions. The people are bewildering, disturbing, fascinating, warped. The play raises severe questions about how we conduct our society. The writing is elegant and eloquent.

Before I was a highway, they all drove right by me.
— *Susan Carlson*

After we discover motion, we must learn to resist the temptation of always trying to move downhill.
— *Michael Skau*

A comic walk-thru festival of the absurd, ALIENS invites you into the world of joys, sorrows, horrors and hopes created in many of us by the onslaught of holiday commercialism. The play also suggests our personal nostalgia for what used to be and what might have been.

CAREER DAY SPOKESPERSON: The Fair Employment Non-discrimination Act has insisted we remove all age restrictions as to who can be a baby. I repeat: each and every one of you can be a baby, regardless of age! We hope you will consider this exciting career choice when it comes time for you to select your life work.

I'm safe. Even with two TV's I still watch less than the U.S. daily household average of seven hours a day. And what about game shows? Does Vanna White perceive of herself as the queen or the pawn?
— *Susan Carlson*

A vivid, bitter transformation play with strong music depicting life and the brutality inside a women's prison. The actors transform back and forth from prisoners — to guards — to visitors — to authority figures. The play is powerful and honest and shows what one must do to survive this experience and remain intact as a human being.

The lattice work spider web structure in BABES IN THE BIGHOUSE is an image of what might be seen as an "eccentric space." The women are both inside and outside this structure, not alternately, but simultaneously. Their bodies are woven in the interstices, the in-between spaces; they look out through the gaps where the web opens. The women are not tangled in the web, their bodies partly constitute it, and yet they are not synonymous with it. They are both same and different.
— Lynda Hart

RONNIE: Listen, you near-sighted Marxist — I chose to be gay! I chose a woman to defy the man. It was a political act and it was a sex act. Trouble with you guys is you got zippers on yer pussies, there's padlocks on the zippers, and you have forgot the combination!

DOCTOR: You act like the worst kind of criminal male, Teresa. You cut another woman's face with a homemade knife! You stole baby pictures from Johanna! You beat Juanita till she had to go to the hospital! If you don't pull yourself together and start to act like a feminine person, you'll get more of these injections.

A witty hybrid of theatre and performance art featuring lovers who love each other as objects.

ANGELA: What do you file?

PEPI: Breasts, bottoms, flesh...

ANGELA: For the company?

PEPI: Energy audits. Little maps of houses from a bird's eye view. The houses glow around the places where energy is escaping into the cold... little glowing auras of sweet hot flesh, long sensuous thermal legs, moist heat mouths, insulated bedroom eyes, heat-pump hair, solarized tongues, double pan-eled hands, throbbing thermostats.

No matter how grotesque or hurt or driven, the face in a frame never ceases to move me. Western aesthetics in a nutshell. — Elin Diamond

SELMA: I set aside one hour each day to exercise my feelings through yearning music. I listen and yearn, and listen and yearn until the tears flow.

SHE: He thinks I'm thinking when he sees those lines deepen, but I'm just trying to see him better.

An economy whose engine is the production of things, theatre, art and spectacle — in other words, everyday life — turns living women and men into irresistibly attractive objects who have almost as much power to arouse and satisfy desires as a brand new, shiny, red Meredes-Benz. — David Savran

This rock musical centers on a group of teenagers who try to organize a positive future. They meet after curfew at a local park, where the "real world" — the worlds of their parents, school, and police, contrast with the world these young people want to create out of their imaginations and faith in the future.

15-year olds imitate typical adult behavior and no one believes it! What if we used doors and windows to invite the world in rather than keep it at a safe distance?
— Susan Carlson

If adulthood means adjusting to a world ruled by the purveyors of useless commodities and the merchants of mass-produced doom, I think I'll stay an adolescent.
— David Savran

IRENE: The fire engine's siren is mine. The fire is yours. The city skyline is mine. The building is yours. The shape of the Mormon Bridge is mine. The suicides are yours. The sweet feel of the air after the rain is mine. The floods are yours. The light patterns on the freeway at night are mine. The drunk drivers are yours. The downy skin of young men is mine. The draft is yours. The beauty of the Sandhills is mine. The MX is yours. The spring piglets are mine. The pork belly is yours. The trees are mine. The electric chair is yours. Hanscom Park is mine. Hiroshima is yours.

This performance piece shows how we label others and package them, according to our preconceptions, into high cholesterol sausages.

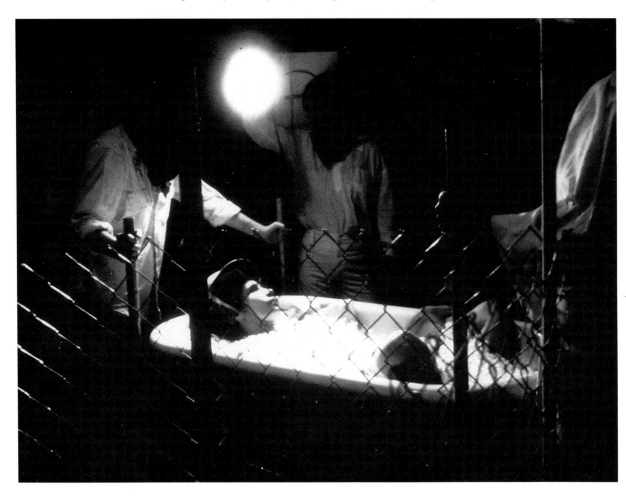

ZULINDA: She's a psychopathic liar who shoplifts. She's a gum snapper, a household engineer. She's an Amazon Warrior.

BUBI: It is the week of boiling things. Your heads shall bob with parsnips in pots of gold.

EDWIN: She's sex crazy. Do you hear me? Last week a redheaded woodpecker got to her and she had to have an abortion. I'm a ventriloquist, not a carpenter, damn it.

Writing with an icepick, Kenneth Bernard frames reality with poetic analysis that would have given cramps to Freud.
— Rochelle Owens

T.S. Eliot said, "This is the way the world ends / not with a bang but a whimper." Eliot was wrong; it ends with a celebration.
— Michael Skau

"Bubi's Hideaway, the nightclub at Armageddon. We love you, we need you. We will have you." This play is a brilliant, vicious metaphor for our decadent society under siege, tougher than any Fassbinder film.

A performance piece starring 50 television sets and one ton of peat moss. Some sets are glowing "blue tubes", some are gutted, some project technicolor humans and some contain living anchor women.

GENDER CASTING/MULTI-CULTURAL CASTING

The company is made up of those willing to commit to the work. Art is about commitment, whatever color — whatever gender. If a script calls for two characters and seven wish to work, the production company becomes seven. If a playwright has envisioned a cast of seventeen but only four company members are committed to the piece, transformational acting skills and visionary design elements empower four performers to fill the stage with seventeen characters.

THE WARMUP IS AN INTEGRATED CREATIVE CENTER EXERCISE

At The Omaha Magic Theatre, we spend 60 minutes warming up before each workshop, rehearsal or performance. Everyone warms up — writers, designers, performers, director, technicians, musicians. Its purpose is to strengthen, center, open and clear the individual as well as create a sense of ensemble. All exercises are breath-based. They serve to warmup the brain, voice, body and sharpen timing.

A spare, realistic and imagistic dramatization of anorexia nervosa as a cultural phenomenon based on historical accounts of "Fasting Girls" (the focus of heated debates between the clergy and the medical community in the 19th century) and on current medical literature which considers the problem to be peculiar to a patriarchal, middle-class, consumer society.

In this surreal exploration of young male attitudes toward sexuality, Virgil a naive farmboy, is told by a beautiful woman in a dream to board the Gray Express and his dreams will come true.

VIRGIL: Your white gossamer gown has me glued to the floor. I can't walk away from you.

Angles of sculptural vision interfaced with human curves become an Indy 500 mind-ride. A visual, emotional and intellectual adventure designed to tickle the lizard brain. This work explores the way humans define themselves, how they perceive *self* and *other* and what channels of communication are opened or closed by those perceptions.

RHODA: Listen, beyond the birds and lawnmowers. Listen, beyond the firecrackers and chewing sounds. Hear from within while enveloped by breath, fur or pine needles.

If imagination were more limited, we could not bear to live; if imagination were any stronger, we would not survive it.
— Michael Skau

In reverie, on the morning of her birth, I and my baby, half human, half whale, swam in tandem across the bottom of the Pacific. The sand scratched our chests, our tails thrust us onward. I tried to tell her that we had to surface but I wasn't able to persuade her. I awoke expecting to find the bed drenched in amniotic fluids. To my confusion the sheets were dry. — Elin Diamond

SKY: They dress their depressed breasts in bulletproof vests while we run naked in the sun.

ZULU: Only a nation of wimps worries about how they look all the time and not what they mean. Think about it.

A multi-dimensional performance event about acute listening. Spines tell jokes while the world breathes her beats. Maybe its time for a romp on all fours.

ZEREO: She bathes in a desert sauna and treats herself with cactus acupuncture.

MISSOURI: This is the sound of your sperm as my ova embraces him.

COLUMBIA: This is the sound of my beautiful blood fertilizing the world.

This wild comedy features an encounter between a successful traveling saleswoman and a man-sized cockroach, a wily seducer who combines the grace of Fred Astaire with the easy charm of David Bowie. Drexler collides Kafka's "Metamorphosis" with Arthur Miller's DEATH OF A SALESMAN to a new comic dimension.

LINDA: Family photographs reveal too much...dear Willy swooning at my feet, for instance. I can't remember whether the photographer suggested it, or whether passion had placed him there, underfoot.

COCKROACH: Look out there, Linda. The world beckons. There's more to consider than you and me. There's street-corner religion. Pimps and prostitutes. The homeless. Everything deep fried in hell. And at night the crunch, crunch, crunch of rats and roaches on the prowl.

Men have antennae that are sensitive to what any woman has to sell. — Michael Skau

MAVIS: I am an ample, substantial, full-bodied, full-figured woman who's finding her voice and her body without your miracle Japanese diets, without your sneering condescension, nutritional ministrations, ablutions, solutions, or dieting resolutions. Even without your acceptance.

For me, these photos — stills — capture the tension between a desire for liberation and the inescapable complicity of those who find themselves contained. We are always already inside the structures that oppress us, as women, as racial and ethnic and sexual minorities.
— *Lynda Hart*

Honest, angry, funny and multi-dimensional. About the liberation of attitudes toward fat and the acceptance of our bodies, no matter what the size.

CLY: We've let them airbrush us into a narrow norm of narrow hips and perky tits.

MAVIS: I don't want my money back. I want my soul. I want to call who I am my own. And who I am isn't some puny-assed, famine victim stick figure swimming in a size 8.

This musical comedy written with love and bitter malice exposes the Holy Order of Divine Illumination. Dramatized by a mother who lived it, here is the story of a family breakup when teenage children join a religious cult whose leader worships broccoli.

ABIGAIL: When I got into Kundalini yoga... When I really got into it... I had the most fantastic orgasms I have ever had in my entire life! You don't need men — when you're makin' it with God, you don't need men at all.

Everyone's fanaticism but our own seems extreme.
— Michael Skau

MRS: Your father and I are trying to choose the best place to send all the library microfilm data of our civilization. Would the moon be safe enough as a repository or should we aim for a galaxy in the Milky Way?

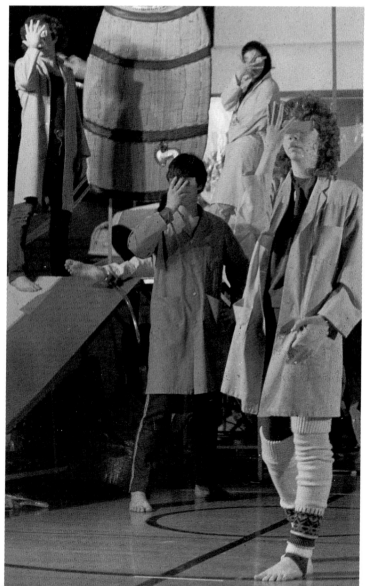

A fast action rock-rap musical dealing with drinking and driving. This explosive play depicts the positive and negative effects of peer pressure, effective decision making, and the rites of passage to adulthood.

CAROL: They served the stuff in garbage cans with floating cigarette butts and coffee grounds on top. But no one seemed to care. They drank it like it was the best thing they ever tasted. And those are the same guys who complain about the cafeteria food!

There is no simple exit. But there are ways of looking out from within — Artaud's "signaling through the flames?"
                                                    — Lynda Hart

Mom and dad can't see us because we're driving into bigger and bigger bottles.   — Jeremy Arakara

A universal indictment of torture covered by four anchor people in a bizarre Brazilian TV station. This news is viewed and abused in the home of an American couple as they engage in kinky sex.

NEWSCASTER TWO: All the possible means of pressure — physical, psychological and moral — are used with increasing sophistication by specialists whose imagination surpasses that of Dante. This is no exaggeration, for as far as we know, no children were tortured in the poet's 'Hell'.

Take one: she's down. Take two: she's still down. Take three: if I have my way, she'll stay down.

The Chinese national sport? — Susan Carlson

Two women and one man create one real and several imaginary
children, then live together in a small apartment. Wry and theatrical, BABY
challenges sexual politics via transformation of ages, genders and
situation to reveal what is really going on between the inner child and our
superimposed adult selves.

*I love to eat my peanut butter painted bread through
plastic baby wrap*　　　　— Jeremy Arakara

CECIL: Grownups think children are little blind beasts who obey. But we're not. Oh no. We have feelings. And we have minds. And that's what's so horrible. When Medea called her boys into the house, they *knew*. They went into the house waiting for the knife.

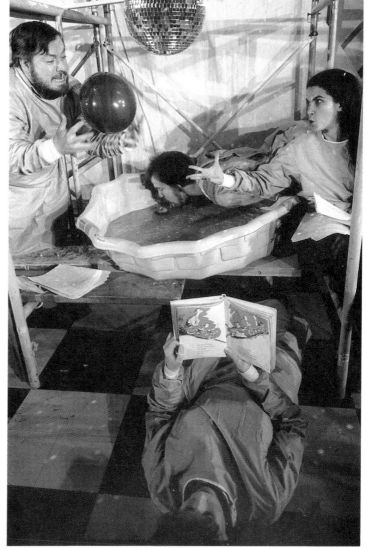

Three American women find themselves
incarcerated during a Contra attack in northern
Nicaragua. Their jailers play the two radicals
off against the *young Republican*. Who's right?
Who's wrong? Who will survive?

NEW THEATRE

The new works we create or present push previously established theatrical boundaries into new dimensions.

We're taught how to set a proper table. "This fork for salad, this knife for butter...now, if you wish, you may use your fingers."

Knowing the rules can free the child to invent, to try out alternatives, to venture into the unknown with confidence.

For the direction and design we begin with what we imagine the writer began with — the theme. We make lists of images — lists and lists of lines, phrases, words; then we transform these lists into conceptual images and sculptural images that can be performed. These may parallel or oppose the themes. Image work is necessary for the original works we create as well as for previously scripted pieces. Some images become part of the piece, others do not. We then integrate our images with the playwright's images and words. Performers take on the task to realize the images in performance.

*High and low are mingled — kings and clowns in-
distinguishable. Even the boundaries between humans
and those "other" animals break down. Is there a hint
of what Donna Haraway names the "cyborg" here?*
— Lynda Hart

JO: Now I know it was just so much theoreti-
cal crap, because here we are and death is
not a concept, it's right outside the door...

JO: There are no heroes, there are no
revolutionary martyrs! There's just you and
me and an M-16, that's it baby!

CHANGE/GROWTH/FLOW

In the late 70's we explored the use of soft-sculpture. This began when audiences responded enthusiastically to the beautiful hand-sewn quilts of our grandmothers used for the set of 100,001 HORROR STORIES OF THE PLAINS. This environment became an art gallery before and after the performance as audience came close to admire and touch. Over the next ten years, environments were sewn. Sometimes characters were added to plays by creating larger-than-life hand-sewn puppets. Some were thin and two dimensional, others were thick multi-dimensional characters on sticks. e.g. RUNNING GAG (lover, husband), GOONA GOONA (the Marriots), KEGGER (Mom and Dad)...Omaha Magic Theatre set design sewing bees created sets, props and puppets. The work represented stitches from crude to refined since each performer had varying degrees of sewing expertise. This communal experience served to reinforce the ensemble and gave "character", an amazing look and feel, to sets and props.

A potluck supper — stories and songs rise up from lantern-lit harvest tables. The settling of the Great Plains is recreated through first-hand accounts, family histories, Midwestern tall tales and genuine tornado survival horror stories.

LYNN: When I was a girl my mother always reminded me of a big ol' icebox — full and big to hold onto and cry on her breasts.

SALTZ: I don't mean to say that going through your first tornado is exactly as good as going through your first feel of loving. But then, if you had it like I had it, honey, you might just prefer the tornado.

He'd turn away after he
hung up the skins to dry,
but the Indian knew...
— Ron Tavel

LABORATORY THEATRE

In a scientific laboratory scientists explore possible cures for cancer or look for a healthier diet, everyone understands that this exploration takes time. Time is required, time is taken. We apply this rule to our developmental work. We try many imaginative alternative approaches. At the Magic Theatre we take our research and development work seriously. Our work for the American theatre is like the research work of engineers, scientists or cancer researchers, without the budget.

a. We keep archival records of direction, script working drafts, design explorations.

b. The creative team meets, and ideas are shared. If a concept doesn't work — we start over.

c. Our focus is not on "schedule" — our focus is on art. Success to us is to be able to work in theatre every day.

We publish and tour many of the works we develop.

New Man and New Woman meet beyond cute, fall in love and get metaphysical.

HE is breakfasted in the cover of his comfortably amusing continuum. SHE wants to think it over. Let's throw a picture on this subject. — Ron Tavel

SHE: You know they say we make agreements to meet before we're even born — but the bitch is that once we do meet we never remember whether the date was for lunch or for life.

HE: So we just have to live in the moment.

SHE: Why does that phrase feel like a girdle?

HE: Oh no, living in the moment isn't a restriction at all, living in the moment is like crotchless panties.

NEWSCASTER FOUR: Personal sensory fulfillment is the safest insurance against yielding to the temptation of unsanctioned unification. It is necessary for a peaceful life to stay in touch with oneself.

The tomorrows of the western world's landscape — where dread and paranoia are capsulized and digested. Terry's imagination delves into monumental themes of present day society.
— Rochelle Owens

The earth's population has increased to the point where we have billions of overcrowded but lonely people.
— Michael Skau

A funny thing happened on the way to the future. People are packed together like sardines and no one can be born until someone dies. In this sci-fi adventure of the emotions, citizens live, work, eat, play, dream, scheme and die in a small cubicle under the constant surveillance of "Central Control".

ROY: Did you sleep?

CYNTHIA: No, but I went traveling in you.

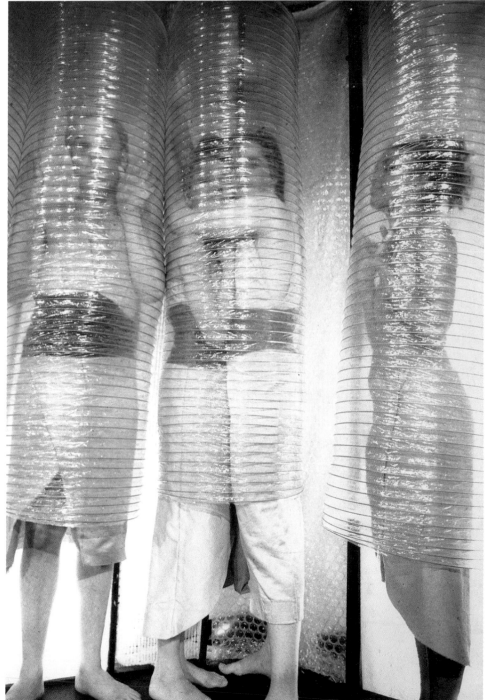

● = *Play titles included in this book.*

All pieces directed by Jo Ann Schmidman unless otherwise noted.

Titles of plays written by more than one playwright are listed under each author; production information is included only once.

Catherine Berg
RR 3, Box 320, Wellsboro, PA

THE BIRTH OF LIMBO DANCING
DATE PRODUCED AT OMT: 3/88
SET DESIGN: BILL FARMER, SORA KIMBERLAIN
& JO ANN SCHMIDMAN
LIGHT DESIGN: JO ANN SCHMIDMAN
MUSIC: JOHN J. SHEEHAN & JONATHAN WARMAN

Jean-Marie Besset
113 West 74 St., #4F, New York, NY 10023

● THE FUNCTION
DATE PRODUCED AT OMT: 2/88
SET DESIGN: BILL FARMER, SORA KIMBERLAIN
& JO ANN SCHMIDMAN
LIGHT DESIGN: JO ANN SCHMIDMAN
MUSIC: JOHN J. SHEEHAN & JONATHAN WARMAN

Ken Bernard
800 Riverside Drive, New York, NY 10032

● NIGHTCLUB
DATE PRODUCED AT OMT: 4/88
SET DESIGN: BILL FARMER, SORA KIMBERLAIN
& JO ANN SCHMIDMAN
LIGHT DESIGN: JO ANN SCHMIDMAN
MUSIC: JOHN J. SHEEHAN & JONATHAN WARMAN

THE UNKNOWN CHINAMAN
DATE PRODUCED AT OMT: 7/71
SET DESIGN: JANE EVANS
LIGHT DESIGN: JANE EVANS
MUSIC: KEN BERNARD
COSTUMES: JO ANN SCHMIDMAN

David Brink
3506 Jackson, #6, Omaha, NE 68105

THE PROGRESSIVE EXAMINATIONS
DATE PRODUCED AT OMT: 8/87
DIRECTION: JO ANN SCHMIDMAN, AMY HARMON,
JOHN J. SHEEHAN & JONATHAN WARMAN
SET DESIGN: DIANE DEGAN
LIGHT DESIGN: JIM SCHUMACHER
COSTUMES: MEGAN TERRY

Jim Celer
P.O. Box 31193, Omaha, NE 68132

● STRANGER THAN SPENDING A NIGHT IN A FT. DODGE TRUCKSTOP
(lyrics by the Ogden Edsel Wahalia Blues Ensemble Mondo Bizzario Band)
DATE PRODUCED AT OMT: 11/72
SET DESIGN: DIANE DEGAN & MEGAN TERRY
LIGHT DESIGN: JUDY GILLESPIE
MUSIC: THE OGDEN EDSEL WAHALIA BLUES ENSEMBLE
MONDO BIZZARIO BAND
COSTUMES: DONALD DUFFY

Constance Congdon
c/o William Morris Agency, Inc., 1350 Avenue of the Americas, New York, NY 10019

TALES OF THE LOST FORMICANS
DATE PRODUCED AT OMT: 8/89
DIRECTION: DEBORAH E. LEECH
SET DESIGN: DIANE DEGAN
LIGHT DESIGN: JIM SCHUMACHER
MUSIC: LARS ERICKSON & FRANK FONG
COSTUMES: JUDE BARRIER

Laura Cosentino
230 West 107 St., #3H, New York, NY 10025

JENNA'S EDGE
DATE PRODUCED AT OMT: 9/87
SET DESIGN: DIANE DEGAN
LIGHT DESIGN: JIM SCHUMACHER
COSTUMES: JO ANN SCHMIDMAN

Migdalia Cruz
99 River Street, New Canaan, CT 06840

● LUCY LOVES ME
DATE PRODUCED AT OMT: 6/89
SET DESIGN: SORA KIMBERLAIN
LIGHT DESIGN: JIM SCHUMACHER
MUSIC: IVY DOW
COSTUMES: JO ANN SCHMIDMAN

Rosalyn Drexler

60-64 Union St., Apt. 1 So., Newark, NJ 07105

● THE BED WAS FULL

DATE PRODUCED AT OMT: 3/88
SET DESIGN: BILL FARMER, SORA KIMBERLAIN
  & JO ANN SCHMIDMAN
LIGHT DESIGN: JO ANN SCHMIDMAN
MUSIC: JOHN J. SHEEHAN & JONATHAN WARMAN
COSTUMES: MEGAN TERRY

● THE HEART THAT EATS ITSELF

DATE PRODUCED AT OMT: 12/88
SET DESIGN: SORA KIMBERLAIN
LIGHT DESIGN: MATT IRVIN
MUSIC: PAKKA KAVAN
COSTUMES: JO ANN SCHMIDMAN

● THE LINE OF LEAST EXISTENCE

DATE PRODUCED AT OMT: 3/87
DIRECTION: MIKE HITZELBERGER
SET DESIGN: BILL FARMER
LIGHT DESIGN: JIM SCHUMACHER
MUSIC: MARK NELSON, FRANK FONG, BILL FARBER
  & ERIC GOOLSBY
COSTUMES: KENDA SLAVIN

● TRANSIENTS WELCOME

(When performed at OMT, called ROOM 17C)
DATE PRODUCED AT OMT: 9/83
SET DESIGN: SORA KIMBERLAIN
LIGHT DESIGN: MARG HEANEY
MUSIC: JOHN J. SHEEHAN
COSTUMES: JANET LIPSEY

Rochelle Holt

59 Sandra Circle, A-3, Westfield, NJ 07090

● WALKING INTO THE DAWN: A CELEBRATION

DATE PRODUCED AT OMT: 12/75
SET DESIGN: DIANE DEGAN
LIGHT DESIGN: COLBERT McCLELLAN
MUSIC: REE SCHONLAU (CERAMIC INSTRUMENTS)
COSTUMES: BARBARA MORRELL

Tom Eyen

C/O Bridget Aschenberg, International Creative
Management, Inc., 40 W. 57 St.,
New York, NY 10019

● WHY HANNA'S SKIRT WON'T STAY DOWN

DATE PRODUCED AT OMT: 2/88
DIRECTION: JO ANN SCHMIDMAN & JOHN J. SHEEHAN
SET DESIGN: BILL FARMER, SORA KIMBERLAIN
  & JO ANN SCHMIDMAN
LIGHT DESIGN: JO ANN SCHMIDMAN
MUSIC: BILL FARBER, JOHN J. SHEEHAN & JONATHAN
  WARMAN

Carol Flint

7970 Woodman Ave., #240, Van Nuys, CA
91402

CLASSICS

DATE PRODUCED AT OMT: 2/88
DIRECTION: JO ANN SCHMIDMAN & JOHN J. SHEEHAN
SET DESIGN: BILL FARMER, SORA KIMBERLAIN
  & JO ANN SCHMIDMAN
LIGHT DESIGN: JO ANN SCHMIDMAN
MUSIC: BILL FARBER, JOHN J. SHEEHAN
  & JONATHAN WARMAN

Maria Irene Fornes

1 Sheridan Square, New York, NY 10014

● MUD

DATE PRODUCED AT OMT: 7/85
DIRECTION: MARIA IRENE FORNES
SET DESIGN: MARIA IRENE FORNES
COSTUMES: MARIA IRENE FORNES & MEG FLAMER

Paul Foster

C/O La Mama ETC, 74A East 4th St.,
New York, NY 10003

TOM PAINE

DATE PRODUCED AT OMT: 6/70
DIRECTION: MICHAEL GRIGGS & LIEBE GRAY
SET DESIGN: DIANE DEGAN
LIGHT DESIGN: LIEBE GRAY

Jone Greenhagen *(Editor)*

2862 Camden Avenue, Omaha NE 68111

● THE NARCO LINGUINI BUST

(with Jo Ann Schmidman & Megan Terry; Lyrics by
Jone Greenhagen, Otis Omaha, John J. Sheehan,
Jo Ann Schmidman, Megan Terry)
DATE PRODUCED AT OMT: 3/74
SET DESIGN: JONE GREENHAGEN
LIGHT DESIGN: COLBERT McCLELLAN
MUSIC: JOHN J. SHEEHAN, JONE GREENHAGEN,
  & OTIS OMAHA
COSTUMES: KATHY MERKEN

Laura Harrington

420 - 7th St., Brooklyn, NY 11215

● ANGEL FACE

DATE PRODUCED AT OMT: 6/89
SET DESIGN: SORA KIMBERLAIN
LIGHT DESIGN: JIM SCHUMACHER
MUSIC: IVY DOW

June Havoc

Rock Spring Farm, 405 Old Long Ridge Rd.,
Stamford, CT 06903

● AN UNEXPECTED EVENING WITH JUNE HAVOC OR BABY JUNE REMEMBERS

DATE PRODUCED AT OMT: 6/84
DIRECTION: JUNE HAVOC
SET DESIGN: JUNE HAVOC
LIGHT DESIGN: JUNE HAVOC
MUSIC: JUNE HAVOC (EDITING AND ARRANGEMENTS)
COSTUMES: JUNE HAVOC

Jean-Claude van Itallie

Box L, Charlemont, MA 01339

THE HUNTER & THE BIRD

DATE PRODUCED AT OMT: 2/88
SET DESIGN: BILL FARMER, SORA KIMBERLAIN
  & JO ANN SCHMIDMAN
LIGHT DESIGN: JO ANN SCHMIDMAN
MUSIC: BILL FARBER & JOHN J. SHEEHAN
COSTUMES: MEGAN TERRY

Judith Katz

P.O. Box 7041, Minneapolis, MN 55407

● TEMPORARY INSANITY

DATE PRODUCED AT OMT: 4/75
SET DESIGN: DIANE DEGAN
LIGHT DESIGN: COLBERT McCLELLAN
MUSIC: JOHN J. SHEEHAN
COSTUMES: MEGAN TERRY

Pakka Kavan

Box 533 CHRB, Saipan, M.P. 96950

● TIX TOX

(with Sora Kimberlain)
DATE PRODUCED AT OMT: 10/80
SET DESIGN: SORA KIMBERLAIN
LIGHT DESIGN: COLBERT McCLELLAN
MUSIC: GAIL HENNIG (ARRANGEMENTS)
COSTUMES: JANET LIPSEY

Sora Kimberlain

505 South 16 St., #1003, Omaha, NE 68102

● BLUE TUBE

(with Jo Ann Schmidman & Megan Terry)
DATE PRODUCED AT OMT: 10/80
SET DESIGN: SORA KIMBERLAIN
LIGHT DESIGN: JO ANN SCHMIDMAN
COSTUMES: JANET LIPSEY

● BODY LEAKS

(with Jo Ann Schmidman & Megan Terry)
DATE PRODUCED AT OMT: 4/90
SET DESIGN: SORA KIMBERLAIN
LIGHT DESIGN: JO ANN SCHMIDMAN
MUSIC: MARIANNE dePURY, LUIGI WAITES
   & MEGAN TERRY
COSTUMES: KENDA SLAVIN & ROBERT N. GILMER
   (JACKETS)

● REFLECTED LIGHT

(with Jo Ann Schmidman & Megan Terry)

● TIX TOX

(with Pakka Kavan)

● WHITE OUT

(with Jo Ann Schmidman & Megan Terry)
DATE PRODUCED AT OMT: 11/80
SET DESIGN: SORA KIMBERLAIN
LIGHT DESIGN: COLBERT McCLELLAN
MUSIC: GAIL HENNIG
COSTUMES: JANET LIPSEY

● YELLOW STRAPPING

(with Jo Ann Schmidman & Megan Terry)
DATE PRODUCED AT OMT: 10/80
SET DESIGN: SORA KIMBERLAIN
LIGHT DESIGN: COLBERT McCLELLAN
MUSIC: GAIL HENNIG
COSTUMES: JANET LIPSEY

Sherry Kramer

2525 Sheridan, Springfield, MO 65804

DAVID'S RED HAIRED DEATH

DATE PRODUCED AT OMT: 9/87
SET DESIGN: DIANE DEGAN
LIGHT DESIGN: JIM SCHUMACHER

Joanna Kraus

Theatre Dept., State University of New York,
College at Brockport, Brockport, NY 14420

TENURE TRACK

(with Greer Woodward)
DATE PRODUCED AT OMT: 8/87
DIRECTION: JO ANN SCHMIDMAN, AMY HARMON,
   JOHN J. SHEEHAN & JONATHAN WARMAN
SET DESIGN: DIANE DEGAN
LIGHT DESIGN: JIM SCHUMACHER

James Larson

Emmy Gifford Theatre, 3504 Center St.,
Omaha, NE 68105

● DINGALING

DATE PRODUCED AT OMT: 8/83
SET DESIGN: SORA KIMBERLAIN
LIGHT DESIGN: MARG HEANEY
MUSIC: JOHN J. SHEEHAN
COSTUMES: JO ANN SCHMIDMAN

● THE GRAY EXPRESS

DATE PRODUCED AT OMT: 3/77
SET DESIGN: DIANE DEGAN
LIGHT DESIGN: JAMES LARSON
MUSIC: NANCY LARSON
COSTUMES: BARBARA MORRELL

Lisa Loomer

2653 Hollyridge Drive, Los Angeles, CA 90068

● NEW AGE ROMANCE

DATE PRODUCED AT OMT: 3/88
SET DESIGN: BILL FARMER, SORA KIMBERLAIN
   & JO ANN SCHMIDMAN
LIGHT DESIGN: JO ANN SCHMIDMAN
MUSIC: JOHN J. SHEEHAN

Mimi Loring

2117 Benson Garden Blvd., Apt 6L,
Omaha, NE 68134

● ASTRAL WHITE

DATE PRODUCED AT OMT: 10/77
SET DESIGN: DIANE DEGAN
LIGHT DESIGN: ELISA STACY
MUSIC: DONNA YOUNG, LYNN HERRICK
   & MECHELLE KELLER
COSTUMES: WES BAILEY & MECHELLE KELLER

Murray Mednick

Padua Hills Playwrights' Workshop Festival,
P.O. Box 4168, Los Angeles, CA 90051-2168

HEADS

DATE PRODUCED AT OMT: 3/91
DIRECTION: JONATHAN WARMAN
SET DESIGN: DIANE DEGAN
LIGHT DESIGN: JONATHAN WARMAN
MUSIC: MIKE BUNGER, DEHNY KNOWLES
COSTUMES: HOLLIE McCLAY

SCAR

DATE PRODUCED AT OMT: 8/87
DIRECTION: JO ANN SCHMIDMAN & AMY HARMON
SET DESIGN: DIANE DEGAN
LIGHT DESIGN: JIM SCHUMACHER

Rochelle Owens

1401 Magnolia, Norman, OK 73072

ISTANBOUL

DATE PRODUCED AT OMT: 9/87
SET DESIGN: DIANE DEGAN
LIGHT DESIGN: JIM SCHUMACHER

● THREE FRONT

DATE PRODUCED AT OMT: 11/88
SET DESIGN: SORA KIMBERLAIN
   & JO ANN SCHMIDMAN
LIGHT DESIGN: MATT IRVIN
MUSIC: PEG SHEEHAN, JOHN J. SHEEHAN
   & RICK HIATT
COSTUMES: MEGAN TERRY

Robert Patrick

C/O La Mama ETC, 74A East 4th St.,
New York, NY 10003

ONE PERSON

DATE PRODUCED AT OMT: 9/87
SET DESIGN: DIANE DEGAN
LIGHT DESIGN: JIM SCHUMACHER
COSTUMES: JONATHAN WARMAN

Charlie Pollock

C/O Bucknell University Alumni Association,
Lewisburg, PA 17837

THE CHICAGO CONSPIRACY TRIAL

DATE PRODUCED AT OMT: 8/71
DIRECTION: FRANK GOODMAN
SET DESIGN: MIKE MIERENDORF
LIGHT DESIGN: MIKE MIERENDORF
COSTUMES: DEBBI WAGNER, CAROL CLARK,
   CAROLYN EVELY & DENISE COCKSON

Terra Daugirda Pressler

4330 Dillard Rd., Eugene, OR 97405

● FAT

DATE PRODUCED AT OMT: 6/89
SET DESIGN: SORA KIMBERLAIN
LIGHT DESIGN: JIM SCHUMACHER
MUSIC: IVY DOW
COSTUMES: MEGAN TERRY

Jo Ann Schmidman

1417 Farnam St., Omaha NE 68102

● ALIENS UNDER GLASS

(with Megan Terry)
DATE PRODUCED AT OMT: 2/82
SET DESIGN: SORA KIMBERLAIN
LIGHT DESIGN: TOM MAZUR
MUSIC: JOHN J. SHEEHAN
COSTUMES: DOROTHY OLESON & MEG FLAMER

● ASTRO*BRIDE

DATE PRODUCED AT OMT: 10/84
SET DESIGN: SORA KIMBERLAIN
MUSIC: JOE BUDENHOLZER, JERRY KAZAKEVICIUS
   & JOHN J. SHEEHAN
COSTUMES: DOROTHY OLESON

● BABES UNCHAINED

(with Megan Terry)
DATE PRODUCED AT OMT: 9/88
SET DESIGN: SORA KIMBERLAIN & BILL FARMER
LIGHT DESIGN: MARGARET MARA
MUSIC: JOHN J. SHEEHAN
COSTUMES: SORA KIMBERLAIN

● BLUE TUBE

(with Sora Kimberlain & Megan Terry)

● BODY LEAKS

(with Sora Kimberlain & Megan Terry)

● THE NARCO LINGUINI BUST

(with Jone Greenhagen & Megan Terry)

● REFLECTED LIGHT

(with Sora Kimberlain & Megan Terry)
DATE PRODUCED AT OMT: 11/80
SET DESIGN: SORA KIMBERLAIN
LIGHT DESIGN: JO ANN SCHMIDMAN
MUSIC: JOHN J. SHEEHAN
COSTUMES: JANET LIPSEY

● RUNNING GAG

(lyrics by Megan Terry)
DATE PRODUCED AT OMT: 1/79
SET DESIGN: DIANE DEGAN & MEGAN TERRY
LIGHT DESIGN: COLBERT McCLELLAN
MUSIC: MARIANNE dePURY & LYNN HERRICK
COSTUMES: ELIZABETH SCHEUERLEIN

● SEA OF FORMS

(with Megan Terry)
DATE PRODUCED AT OMT: 9/86
SET DESIGN: BILL FARMER
LIGHT DESIGN: JIM SCHUMACHER
MUSIC: JOE BUDENHOLZER, JOHN J. SHEEHAN,
   MARK NELSON & IVY DOW
COSTUMES: KENDA SLAVIN

● WALKING THROUGH WALLS

(with Megan Terry)
DATE PRODUCED AT OMT: 11/87
SET DESIGN: BILL FARMER
LIGHT DESIGN: CHUCK ST. LUCAS
MUSIC: BILL FARBER, MARK NELSON
   & JOHN J. SHEEHAN
COSTUMES: MEGAN TERRY

● WHITE OUT

(with Sora Kimberlain & Megan Terry)

● X-RAYED-IATE: E-MOTION IN ACTION

(with Megan Terry)
DATE PRODUCED AT OMT: 5/84
SET DESIGN: SORA KIMBERLAIN
LIGHT DESIGN: JO ANN SCHMIDMAN
MUSIC: JOHN J. SHEEHAN, JOE BUDENHOLZER
   & JERRY KAZAKEVICIUS

● YELLOW STRAPPING

(with Sora Kimberlain & Megan Terry)

John J. Sheehan

416 Bancroft Ave., Omaha, NE 68108

A LOOP IN TIME

(lyrics by Megan Terry)
DATE PRODUCED AT OMT: 8/73
DIRECTION: JO ANN SCHMIDMAN & JOHN J. SHEEHAN
SET DESIGN: JOHN J. SHEEHAN
LIGHT DESIGN: COLBERT McCLELLAN
MUSIC: JOHN J. SHEEHAN

Production History

Sam Shepard

C/O Lois Berman, 240 W. 44th St.,
New York, NY 10036

CHICAGO

DATE PRODUCED AT OMT: 9/87
SET DESIGN: DIANE DEGAN
LIGHT DESIGN: JIM SCHUMACHER

Kat Smith

149 West 72, #3A, New York, NY 10023

● **CONSEQUENCE**

DATE PRODUCED AT OMT: 2/88
DIRECTION: JO ANN SCHMIDMAN & JOHN J. SHEEHAN
SET DESIGN: BILL FARMER, SORA KIMBERLAIN
& JO ANN SCHMIDMAN
LIGHT DESIGN: JO ANN SCHMIDMAN
MUSIC: BILL FARBER, JOHN J. SHEEHAN
& MARK NELSON
COSTUMES: MEGAN TERRY

Susan Harris Smith

6208 Howe Street, Pittsburgh, PA 15206

● **DEAD WEIGHT**

DATE PRODUCED AT OMT: 6/91
DIRECTION: WILLIAM YORK HYDE & HOLLIE McCLAY
SET DESIGN: WILLIAM YORK HYDE & HOLLIE McCLAY
LIGHT DESIGN: WILLIAM YORK HYDE & HOLLIE McCLAY

Ron Tavel

528 Gov. Nicholls, New Orleans, LA 70116

● **KITCHENETTE**

DATE PRODUCED AT OMT: 3/88
SET DESIGN: BILL FARMER, SORA KIMBERLAIN
& JO ANN SCHMIDMAN
LIGHT DESIGN: JO ANN SCHMIDMAN
MUSIC: JOHN J. SHEEHAN
COSTUMES: MEGAN TERRY

● **MY FOETUS LIVED ON AMBOY STREET**

DATE PRODUCED AT OMT: 10/88
SET DESIGN: SORA KIMBERLAIN, JO ANN SCHMIDMAN
& IVY DOW (SPIDER DESIGN)
LIGHT DESIGN: MATT IRVIN
MUSIC: JOHN J. SHEEHAN, CATHERINE BERG
& SHULI RAYBERG
COSTUMES: JO ANN SCHMIDMAN

Megan Terry

1417 Farnam St., Omaha, NE 68102

● **ALIENS UNDER GLASS**

(with Jo Ann Schmidman)

● **AMERICAN KING'S ENGLISH FOR QUEENS**

DATE PRODUCED AT OMT: 3/78
SET DESIGN: DIANE DEGAN & ELISA STACY
LIGHT DESIGN: ELISA STACY
MUSIC: LYNN HERRICK
COSTUMES: MECHELLE KELLER, ELISA STACY
& DENNIS MURPHY

● **AMTRAK**

DATE PRODUCED AT OMT: 2/88
SET DESIGN: BILL FARMER, SORA KIMBERLAIN
& JO ANN SCHMIDMAN
LIGHT DESIGN: JO ANN SCHMIDMAN
MUSIC: JOHN J. SHEEHAN & JONATHAN WARMAN
COSTUMES: MEGAN TERRY

● **BABES IN THE BIGHOUSE**

DATE PRODUCED AT OMT: 11/74
SET DESIGN: DIANE DEGAN
LIGHT DESIGN: COLBERT McCLELLAN
MUSIC: JOHN J. SHEEHAN
COSTUMES: MEGAN TERRY

● **BABES UNCHAINED**

(with Jo Ann Schmidman)

● **BLUE TUBE**

(with Sora Kimberlain & Jo Ann Schmidman)

● **BODY LEAKS**

(with Sora Kimberlain & Jo Ann Schmidman)

● **BRAZIL FADO**

DATE PRODUCED AT OMT: 1/77
DIRECTION: JOE GUINAN
SET DESIGN: DIANE DEGAN
LIGHT DESIGN: JAMES LARSON
MUSIC: JUDITH KATZ & NANCY LARSON

CHOOSE A SPOT ON THE FLOOR

(with Jo Ann Schmidman)
DATE PRODUCED AT OMT: 6/72
SET DESIGN: DIANE DEGAN
LIGHT DESIGN: COLBERT McCLELLAN
MUSIC: ANN McMILLAN, CAPTAIN HUNGRY
& THE MUNCHIES

● **DINNER'S IN THE BLENDER**

DATE PRODUCED AT OMT: 4/86
SET DESIGN: DIANE OSTDIEK & COLIN C. SMITH
LIGHT DESIGN: JIM SCHUMACHER
MUSIC: JOE BUDENHOLZER & JOHN J. SHEEHAN
COSTUMES: MEGAN TERRY

● **15 MILLION 15 YEAR-OLDS**

DATE PRODUCED AT OMT: 8/83
SET DESIGN: SORA KIMBERLAIN
LIGHT DESIGN: MARG HEANEY
MUSIC: JOE BUDENHOLZER & JOHN J. SHEEHAN
COSTUMES: SUSAN CROFT, JANIS WHITE,
JILL ANDERSON, JED CHRYSLER,
JO ANN SCHMIDMAN & THE COMPANY

● **FUTURE SOAP**

DATE PRODUCED AT OMT: 5/87
DIRECTION: GERALD OSTDIEK
SET DESIGN: DANIEL SHEPARD & JUDITH SHEPARD
LIGHT DESIGN: JIM SCHUMACHER
MUSIC: BILL FARBER, FRANK FONG, ERIC GOOLSBY
& MARK NELSON
COSTUMES: KENDA SLAVIN

● **GOONA GOONA**

DATE PRODUCED AT OMT: 11/79
SET DESIGN: MEGAN TERRY
LIGHT DESIGN: COLBERT McCLELLAN
MUSIC: LYNN HERRICK
COSTUMES: MEGAN TERRY

● **HEADLIGHTS**

DATE PRODUCED AT OMT: 4/89
SET DESIGN: SORA KIMBERLAIN & BILL FARMER
LIGHT DESIGN: JO ANN SCHMIDMAN
& JIM SCHUMACHER
MUSIC: FRANK FONG, REX GRAY, RICK HIATT,
LORI LOREE, MARK NELSON & LUIGI WAITES
COSTUMES: KENDA SLAVIN

● **KEGGER**
(additional lyrics by Del Johnson)
DATE PRODUCED AT OMT: 9/82 AND 3/85
DIRECTION: ('82) SCHMIDMAN; ('85) SHARON ROSS
SET DESIGN: NEBRASKA DEPT. OF HIGHWAY SAFETY,
   JO ANN SCHMIDMAN, JOE BUDENHOLZER, SOUTH
   OMAHA BOYS CLUB; JULI BURNEY & DICK GRUBE
   (SOFT-SCULPTURE)
MUSIC: MARIANNE dePURY & JOE BUDENHOLZER

● **THE NARCO LINGUINI BUST**
(with Jone Greenhagen & Jo Ann Schmidman)

● **OBJECTIVE LOVE**
DATE PRODUCED AT OMT: 12/80
SET DESIGN: SORA KIMBERLAIN & MEGAN TERRY
LIGHT DESIGN: JO ANN SCHMIDMAN
MUSIC: JOHN J. SHEEHAN
COSTUMES: JANET LIPSEY

● **100,001 HORROR STORIES OF THE PLAINS**
(Edited by Megan Terry; Written by the People of Nebraska, Iowa, Kansas and South Dakota)
DATE PRODUCED AT OMT: 11/76
SET DESIGN: DIANE DEGAN
LIGHT DESIGN: ELISA STACY
MUSIC: NANCY LARSON
COSTUMES: BARBARA MORRELL & E. A. DOUGLASS

THE PIONEER
DATE PRODUCED AT OMT: 3/74

● **PRO-GAME**
DATE PRODUCED AT OMT: 1/77
DIRECTION: JUDITH KATZ
SET DESIGN: DIANE DEGAN
LIGHT DESIGN: JAMES LARSON
MUSIC: JO ANN SCHMIDMAN
COSTUMES: JO ANN SCHMIDMAN

● **REFLECTED LIGHT**
(with Sora Kimberlain & Jo Ann Schmidman)

● **SEA OF FORMS**
(with Jo Ann Schmidman)

● **SLEAZING TOWARD ATHENS**
DATE PRODUCED AT OMT: 6/86
DIRECTION: MICHELLE HENSLEY
SET DESIGN: COLIN C. SMITH
LIGHT DESIGN: FRANK XAVIER KOSMICKI
MUSIC: JOE BUDENHOLZER & JOHN J. SHEEHAN

THE TOMMY ALLEN SHOW: OMAHA
DATE PRODUCED AT OMT: 6/70
DIRECTION: LIEBE GRAY
LIGHT DESIGN: LIEBE GRAY
MUSIC: FRANK YOUNGBLOOD
COSTUMES: JO ANN SCHMIDMAN

● **WALKING THROUGH WALLS**
(with Jo Ann Schmidman)

● **WHITE OUT**
(with Sora Kimberlain & Jo Ann Schmidman)

● **YELLOW STRAPPING**
(with Sora Kimberlain & Jo Ann Schmidman)

● **X-RAYED-IATE: E-MOTION IN ACTION**
(with Jo Ann Schmidman)

Kathleen Tolan
C/O Joyce Ketay, 320 West 90th St.,
New York, NY 10024

DIGGING TO CHINA
(When performed at OMT, called SEQUENCES)
DATE PRODUCED AT OMT: 7/81
DIRECTION: KATHLEEN TOLAN
SET DESIGN: LES DAVIS, JO ANN SCHMIDMAN,
   EVE FELDER & C. L. PROCHAZKA
LIGHT DESIGN: MORGAN MICHAELS
COSTUMES: THE COMPANY

Paula Vogel
Playwriting Program, Box 1852,
Brown University, Providence RI 02912

● **AND BABY MAKES SEVEN**
DATE PRODUCED AT OMT: 3/88
SET DESIGN: BILL FARMER, SORA KIMBERLAIN
   & JO ANN SCHMIDMAN
LIGHT DESIGN: JO ANN SCHMIDMAN
MUSIC: JOHN J. SHEEHAN & JONATHAN WARMAN
COSTUMES: JO ANN SCHMIDMAN

Greer Woodward
350 - 65 St., Apt. 14M, Brooklyn, NY 11220

TENURE TRACK
(with Joanna Kraus)

Susan Yankowitz
205 W. 89th St., #8F, New York, NY 10024

TRANSPLANT
DATE PRODUCED AT OMT: 2/71
DIRECTION: RAYMOND G. GLASS
SET DESIGN: KAT KAISER
LIGHT DESIGN: KAT KAISER
MUSIC: TOM MINTHORN
COSTUMES: KAT KAISER

● **ALARMS**
DATE PRODUCED AT OMT: 11/88
SET DESIGN: SORA KIMBERLAIN
   & JO ANN SCHMIDMAN
LIGHT DESIGN: MATT IRVIN
MUSIC: IVY DOW, JOHN J. SHEEHAN, CATHERINE BERG
   & SHULI RAYBERG
COSTUMES: MEGAN TERRY & JO ANN SCHMIDMAN

Production History

These performers appear in the production photos:

Jill Anderson

Gwen Andrews

Thomas Arnold

Brian Bengtson

Genevieve Andrews-Bennett

Catherine Berg

Eli Berry

Pat Blanchet

Steve Booton

Tammy Brown

Joe Budenholzer

Chris Button

Jim Celar

Susan Croft

Jed Chrysler

Ivy Dow

Jeanne Dow

Margie Du Be

Kermit Dunkelberg

Vince Egan

Bill Farmer

Eve Felder

David Fiedler

Don Fiedler

Ann Filemyr

Bill Frenzer

Jone Greenhagen

June Havoc

Gail Hennig

Lynn Herrick

Rick Hiatt

Frank Fong

Robert N. Gilmer

Star Graham

Mary S. Green

Joe Guinan

Amy Harmon

Mike Hitzelberge

William York Hyde

Matt Irvin

Mark Jarecke

Wendell Jon

Judith Katz

Pakka Kavan

Jane Keller

Mechelle Keller

Sora Kimberlain

Phyllis Kohl

Frank Xavier Kosmicki

Krystal Kremla

Keri Kripal

Jim LaFerla

Charles Larson

James Larson

Nancy Larson

Brett Lassiter

Alberto Leal

Gracie Lee

Deborah E. Leech

Jon Lindley

Barbara Loper

Michael Malstead

Teresa Marsh

Craig McCurry

Hollie McClay

Tom McLaughlin

Evelyn McLellan

Dylan Mitchell

Frank Novak

Diane Ostdiek

Craig Perkins

Gary Planck

Aaron Pollak

C. L. Prochazka

Shuli Rayberg

Roger Reeves

Heather Rehurek

Hilary Rehurek

Jerry Reynolds

Benjamin Richards

Jo Ann Schmidman

Rae Ann Schmitz

John J. Sheehan

Daniel Shepard

Jennifer Shepard

Kevin Shoesmith

Lonnie Snipes

Todd Starlin

Megan Terry

Mary Thatcher

Tim Thompson

James Thorn

Otis 12

Kate Ullman

Jonathan Warman

Susan Watts

Peggy Aufenkamp Wheeler

Janis White

Russell Williams

Kimberly Wright

Jennifer Yarns

Donna Young

Magic Theatre Creative Team

Megan Terry is Literary Manager, Playwright-in-Residence, Performer, Composer and Photographer for the Omaha Magic Theatre Company. She is an internationally acclaimed playwright and has published more than 50 plays. Helene Keyssar in Feminist Theatre names her "the mother of feminist theatre." A founding member of the Open Theatre, New York Theatre Strategy and the Women's Theatre Council, Terry has been awarded every major grant or fellowship for playwriting. Her work has been translated into every major language and is produced internationally.

Jo Ann Schmidman is Artistic/Producing Director of the Omaha Magic Theatre which she founded in 1968. She is a Performer, Writer and Designer for the Company. She was a co-creator/performer in the award-winning Open Theatre and performed throughout the world. Her play Running Gag was commissioned to perform for the world's athletes at the 1980 Winter Olympics. Schmidman guides artist contributions and the multidisciplinary development of both scripted and original works. She is a noted director of workshops, integrated body and voice warm-ups, avant garde performance and is a charismatic lecturer on theatre.

Sora Kimberlain, a multi-talented painter, sculptor and designer is renowned for the creation of large scale installations emphasizing sculpture, light and projection. Kimberlain is a Performer, Writer and Designer for the Magic Theatre Company, where she also designs and executes window installations and performance environments. She received a Rockefeller Foundation Grant (writer/designer); was co-founder of Lovensko (visual arts collective), YUR Studio/Gallery, Eclectic Cooperative Artist Gallery and Co-Founder/Editor of Beef tabloid. Her work has been exhibited in museums, galleries, and private collections.

Photo Respondents

Jeremy Arakara is an independent, international theatre observer and music-theatre composer.

Susan Carlson is Associate Professor of English at Iowa State University, where she teaches drama. She serves as a member of The Women's Studies Program Committee at Iowa State, as a Reviewer for St. Martin's Press, and Reader for Essays in Literature. Her new book, Women and Comedy: Rewriting the British Theatrical Tradition, joins a long list of publication credits including Women of Grace: Henry James's Plays and the Comedy of Manners.

Migdalia Cruz This playwright has accumulated an impressive list of productions in the last two years. Her talent has been recognized and nurtured by the Sundance Institute, Centre D'Essai, Maria Irene Fornes's Playwright's Laboratory and the New Play Festival at the Mark Taper Forum. She has received commissions from the American Musical Theatre Festival, Theatre For A New Audience, INTAR, RAICES and DUO.

Elin Diamond, Associate Professor of English at Rutgers University, has contributed numerous articles to major theatre journals and lectured extensively throughout the nation. The author of Pinter's Comic Play, she is currently writing Feminist Stagings: Unmaking Mimesis, to be published by Routledge. She says, "This study is an intertextual reading of feminist, dramatic and performance theory and plays by selected dramatists from Aphra Behn to Simone Benmussa."

Jill Dolan is an Assistant Professor in the Department of Theatre and Drama at the University of Wisconsin - Madison. She is the author of The Feminist Spectator as Critic and co-editor with Brooks McNamara of The Drama Review: 30 Years of Writing on the Avant-Garde. She has published feminist performance criticism and theory in Theatre Journal, Drama Review, Journal of Popular Culture and Art & Cinema.

Lynda Hart is Assistant Professor of English at the University of Pennsylvania. Her teaching and research interests are modern/contemporary drama and feminism in theatre. She is author of Sam Shepard's Metaphorical Stages and is currently editing a new book with Peggy Phelan, Acting Out: Feminist Performances. She also edited the book Making A Spectacle, published by University of Michigan Press.

Rochelle Owens, a playwright, poet, translator, critic and writer of short fiction has been widely published in all of these capacities. There are fifteen collections of her poems and plays. A pioneer in the experimental Off-Broadway theatre movement, Ms. Owens was instrumental in changing the face of American Theatre. She has received several Village Voice Obie Awards and honors from the New York Drama Critics' Circle. She currently teaches poetry at the University of Oklahoma, Norman.

David Savran is Assistant Professor of English at Brown University, Providence, RI. He has written numerous articles for the field and two recent books: In Their Own Words: Contemporary American Playwrights and Breaking the Rules: The Wooster Group, both published by Theatre Communications Group, NYC. He has directed theatre productions in the US and Canada.

Michael Skau, Professor of English, University of Nebraska - Omaha, is best known for his incisive and warm-spirited poetry. Over sixty of his poems have been published in Poetry Journals, Art Magazines and Newspapers. Professor Skau's newest collection of poetry is entitled Me and God. His numerous publication credits include the book Constantly Risking Absurdity: The Writings of Lawrence Ferlinghetti.

Ronald Tavel, writer of the legendary Gorilla Queen, founded and named the Ridiculous Theatre Movement. He had worked as Andy Warhol's scenarist, writing, directing and acting in a score of films. He was Playwright-in-Residence at Playhouse of the Ridiculous and Lee Strasberg's Actor's Studio. Among the many grants he has won are Rockefeller, Guggenheim, and a National Endowment for the Arts Playwriting Fellowship.